SMART
ABOUT
SPORTS

Meet
the
Cardinals

By
Mike Kennedy
with Mark Stewart

NORWOODHOUSE PRESS

Norwood House Press, P.O. Box 316598, Chicago, Illinois 60631

For information regarding Norwood House Press,
please visit our website at: www.norwoodhousepress.com or call 866-565-2900.

Photo Credits:
  Associated Press (4, 21, 22), Getty Images (7, 8, 12, 13, 15, 16), Black Book Partners (18, 23 both),
  Icon SMI (20).
Cover Photos:
  Top Left: Topps, Inc.; Top Right: Dilip Vishwanat/Getty Images; Bottom Left: AP Photo/Morry Gash; Bottom
  Right: Topps, Inc.
The baseball memorabilia photographed for this book is part of the authors' collection:
  Page 6) St. Louis Cardinals Stadium Pin, Page 10) Rogers Hornsby: Golden Press; Stan Musial: Red Heart Dog
  Food; Dizzy Dean: Gold Medal Flour/General Mills, Inc.; Bob Gibson: Topps, Inc., Page 11) Lou Brock: Topps,
  Inc.; Ozzie Smith: Donruss Trading Card Company/Panini; Willie McGree: Topps, Inc.; Albert Pujols: Topps, Inc.
Special thanks to Topps, Inc.

Editor: Brian Fitzgerald
Designer: Ron Jaffe
Project Management: Black Book Partners, LLC.
Editorial Production: Jessica McCulloch

LIBRARY OF CONGRESS CATALOGING-IN-PUBLICATION DATA
    Kennedy, Mike (Mike William), 1965-
    Meet the Cardinals / by Mike Kennedy with Mark Stewart.
       p. cm. -- (Smart about sports)
    Includes bibliographical references and index.
    Summary: "An introductory look at the St. Louis Cardinals baseball team.
    Includes a brief history, facts, photos, records, glossary, and fun
    activities"--Provided by publisher.
    ISBN-13: 978-1-59953-373-5 (library edition : alk. paper)
    ISBN-10: 1-59953-373-1 (library edition : alk. paper)
    1. St. Louis Cardinals (Baseball team)--Juvenile literature. I. Stewart,
    Mark, 1960- II. Title.
    GV875.S74K46 2010
    796.357'640977866--dc22
                                        2009043319

Manufactured in the United States of America in North Mankato, Minnesota.
N147—012010

Contents

Words in **bold type** are defined on page 24.

Adam Wainwright and his teammates celebrate their 2006 championship.

The
St. Louis Cardinals

Have you ever watched a cardinal closely? It is a bright and colorful bird. It is also brave and tough. The more you watch the St. Louis Cardinals play, the more their name fits. The Cardinals play smart and exciting baseball. They also love a good, tough game!

Once Upon a Time

The Cardinals are one of the oldest teams in baseball. They joined the National League (NL) in 1892. Baseball is very popular in St. Louis. For many years, there were two teams in town!

The Cardinals have always put great players on the field. Their famous hitters include Rogers Hornsby, Joe Medwick, 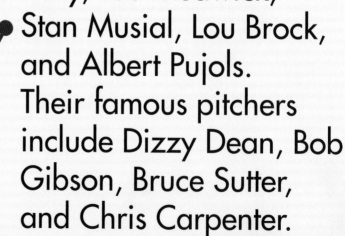 Stan Musial, Lou Brock, and Albert Pujols. Their famous pitchers include Dizzy Dean, Bob Gibson, Bruce Sutter, and Chris Carpenter.

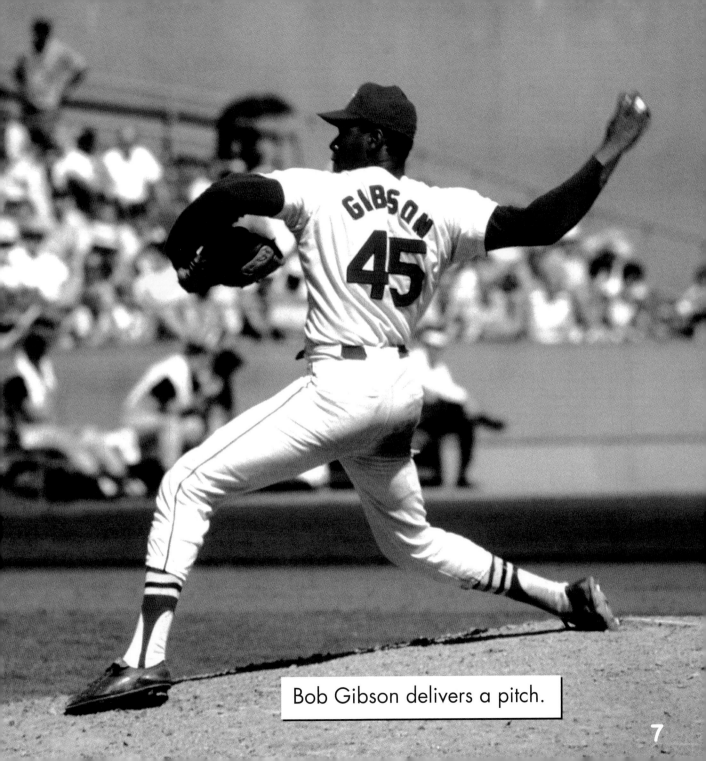

Bob Gibson delivers a pitch.

The Gateway Arch stands tall behind Busch Stadium.

At the Ballpark

The Cardinals play their home
games in Busch Stadium. It is
named after the family that
owned the team for many years.
Every seat in the ballpark has
a good view of the field. From
most seats, fans can see the
famous Gateway Arch.

Shoe Box

The cards on these pages belong to the authors. They show some of the best Cardinals ever.

ROGERS HORNSBY
second base

Rogers Hornsby

Second Baseman

- **1915–1926 & 1933**
Rogers Hornsby was the NL batting champion six years in a row. Some say he was the best right-handed hitter ever.

STAN MUSIAL
ST. LOUIS CARDINALS

Stan Musial

Outfielder/First Baseman

- **1941–1963**
Stan Musial was the NL Most Valuable Player (MVP) three times. "Stan the Man" had 475 home runs and 3,630 hits for the Cardinals.

Dizzy Dean

Pitcher

- **1930 & 1932–1937**
Dizzy Dean was funny and friendly. He also had a great fastball. He was the last NL pitcher to win 30 games in a season.

Bob Gibson

Pitcher • 1959–1975
When there was an important game to pitch, no one was better than Bob Gibson. He was MVP of the World Series twice.

GIBSON

10

Lou Brock

Outfielder • 1964–1979
Lou Brock was a fast and daring runner. He led the league in stolen bases eight times.

Ozzie Smith

Shortstop • 1982–1996
Ozzie Smith was called the "Wizard of Oz" because of his magical fielding. He was one of the most popular players in baseball.

Willie McGee

Outfielder

• 1982–1990 & 1996–1999
Willie McGee was an exciting runner, hitter, and fielder. In 1985, he led the NL with 18 triples and was named league MVP.

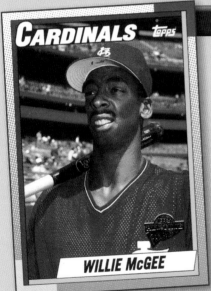

Albert Pujols

First Baseman • 2001–
Every year, Albert Pujols was one of baseball's best hitters. He was always among the NL leaders in **batting average**, home runs, and **runs batted in**.

ABC's of Baseball

In this picture of Chris Carpenter, how many things can you find that start with the letter **C**?

See page 23 for answer.

Brain Games

Here is a poem about a great St. Louis star:

There once was a Cardinal named Brock,
Whose speed was just too fast to clock.
It was never a race
When Lou stole a base.
Opponents just stood there in shock.

Guess which one of these facts is **TRUE**:

- *Lou owned a flower shop in St. Louis.*
- *Lou wore his hair in a ponytail and tucked it under his cap.*

See page 23 for answer.

Lou Brock loved to steal bases.

Fredbird is ready to field a grounder.

Fun on the Field

One of the first things that fans see at a Cardinals game is Fredbird. Fredbird is the team's mascot. He roams through the stands so he can meet the fans. Fredbird also goes on the field. The players and umpires love to joke with him between innings.

On the Map

The Cardinals call St. Louis, Missouri home. Their players come from all over the country—and all over the world. Match these MVPs with the places they were born:

 **Frankie Frisch** • **1931 NL MVP**
Bronx, New York

 **Stan Musial**
• 1943, 1946 & 1948 NL MVP
Donora, Pennsylvania

 **Orlando Cepeda** • **1967 NL MVP**
Ponce, Puerto Rico

 **Bob Gibson** • **1968 NL MVP**
Omaha, Nebraska

 **Keith Hernandez**
• 1979 NL MVP
San Francisco, California

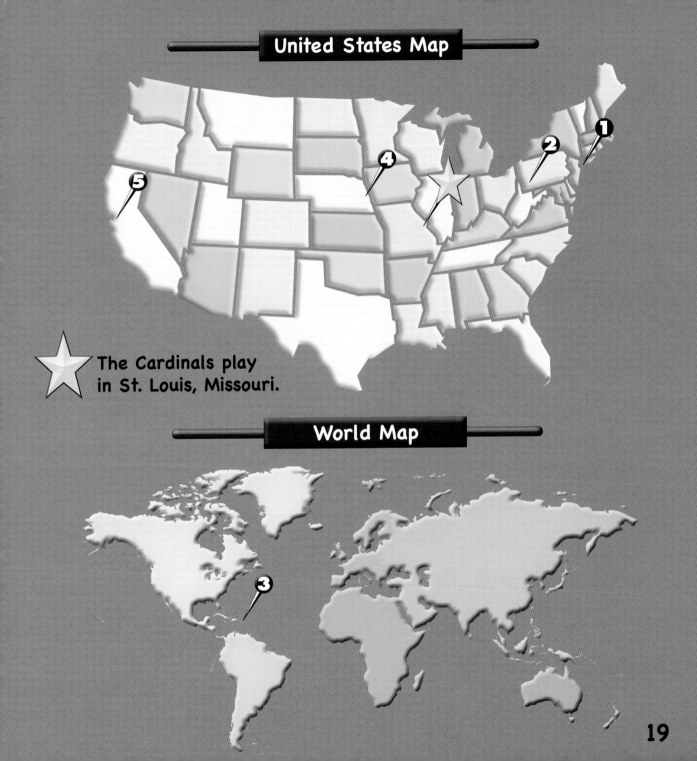

United States Map

World Map

The Cardinals play
in St. Louis, Missouri.

19

What's in the Locker?

Baseball teams wear different uniforms for home games and away games. The St. Louis home uniform is bright white. The uniform top shows two cardinals on a bat. **C-A-R-D-I-N-A-L-S** is spelled out in script letters.

Yadier Molina wears the team's home uniform.

The St. Louis away
uniform is gray. It also
shows the cardinals
and the bat. The
team's cap has the
letters **S-T-L**, which is
short for "St. Louis."
The Cardinals wear
a red cap at home
and a blue cap on
the road.

Albert Pujols wears the team's
road uniform.

We Won!

The Cardinals won their first World Series in 1926. They won their 10th in 2006. The Cardinals never give up. The bigger the game, the better they play.

In 1946, the Cardinals beat the Boston Red Sox in the World Series. They won Game 7 when Enos Slaughter scored all the way from first base on a hit to the outfield. Slaughter's daring run is one of baseball's most famous plays ever.

Enos Slaughter scores the winning run in the 1946 World Series.

Record Book

These Cardinals stars set amazing team records.

Hitter	Record	Year
Rogers Hornsby	250 Hits	1922
Joe Medwick	64 Doubles	1936
Mark McGwire	70 Home Runs	1998

Pitcher	Record	Year
Bob Gibson	13 **Shutouts**	1968
Lee Smith	47 **Saves**	1991
Jason Isringhausen	47 Saves	2004

Answer for ABC's of Baseball

Here are words in the picture that start with **C:**
Cap, Cardinal, Cheek, Chin, Chris Carpenter.
Did you find any others?

Answer for Brain Games

*The first fact is true. Lou Brock owned a flower shop
in St. Louis. He stole 888 bases in his 16 seasons
with the Cardinals.*

Baseball Words

BATTING AVERAGE
A measure of how often a batter gets a hit. A .300 average is very good.

RUNS BATTED IN
The number of runners that score on a batter's hits and walks.

SAVES
A number that shows how many times a pitcher comes into a game and completes a win for his team.

SHUTOUTS
A number that shows how many times a pitcher goes an entire game without giving up a run.

Index

Photos are on **bold** numbered pages.

About the Cardinals

Learn more about the Cardinals at stlouis.cardinals.mlb.com

Learn more about baseball at www.baseballhalloffame.org